How To Draw Realistic Skulls Volume 7

Simple Guide to Drawing Skulls

How to Draw Skulls

By : Gala Publication

2

Published By :

Gala Publication

© Copyright 2015 – Gala Publication

ISBN-13: **978-1522786030**
ISBN-10: **1522786031**

Table of Contents

4

DEER SKULL

STEP 1

STEP 2

STEP 3

STEP 4

STEP 5

STEP 6

GAMBLER SKULL

STEP 1

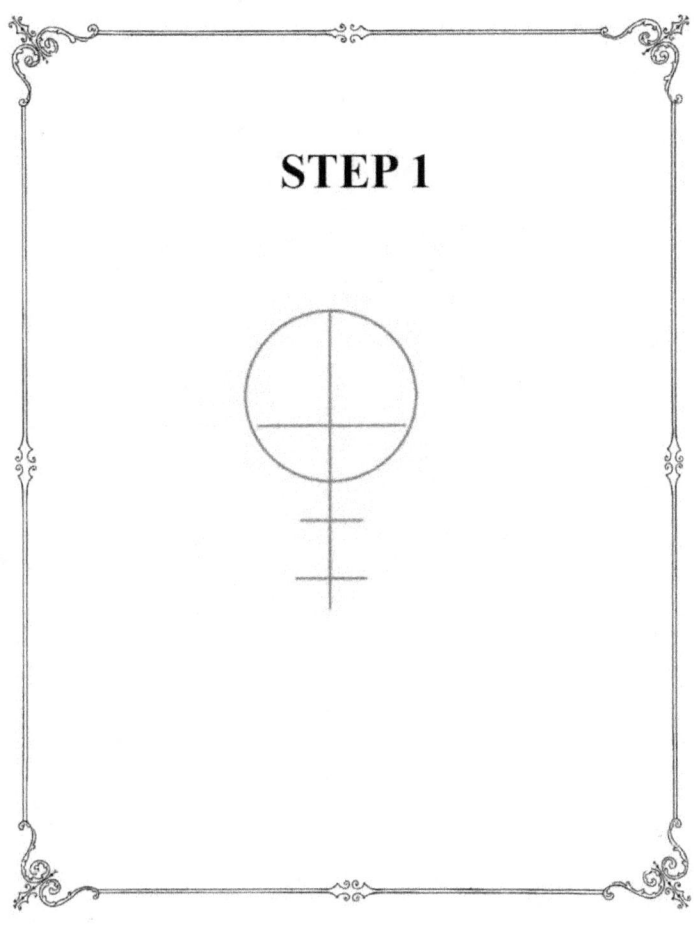

STEP 2

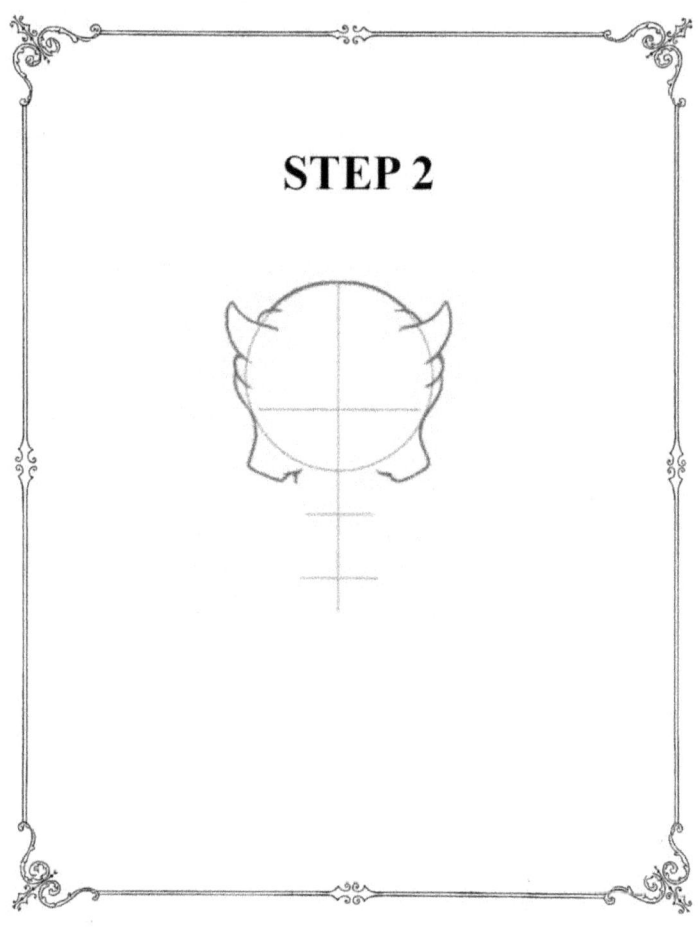

STEP 3

STEP 4

STEP 5

STEP 6

HIPPIE SKULL

STEP 1

STEP 2

STEP 3

STEP 4

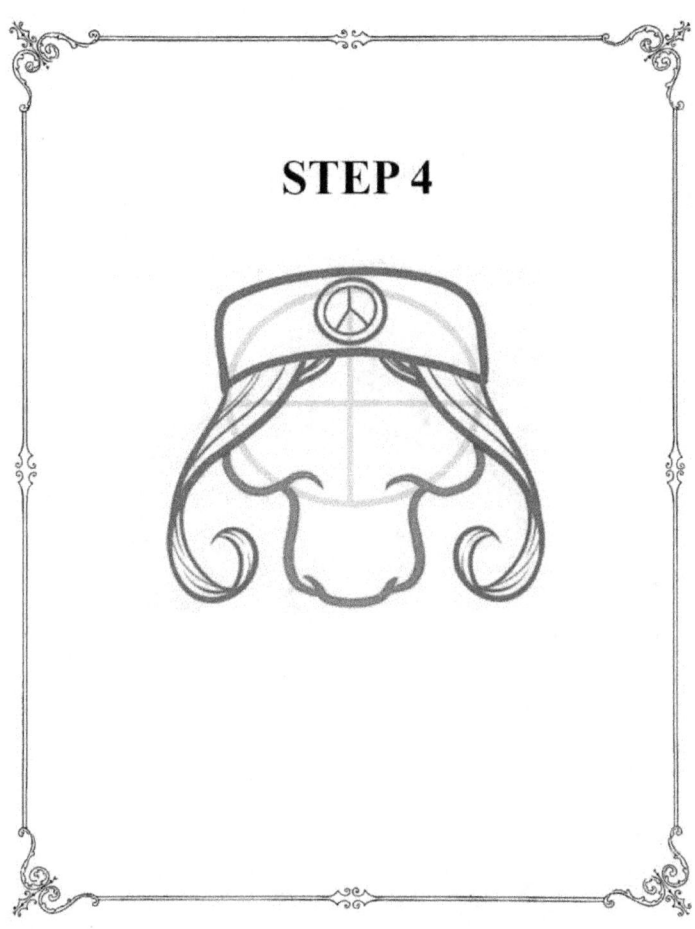

STEP 5

STEP 6

STEP 7

STEP 8

ROSE SKULL

STEP 1

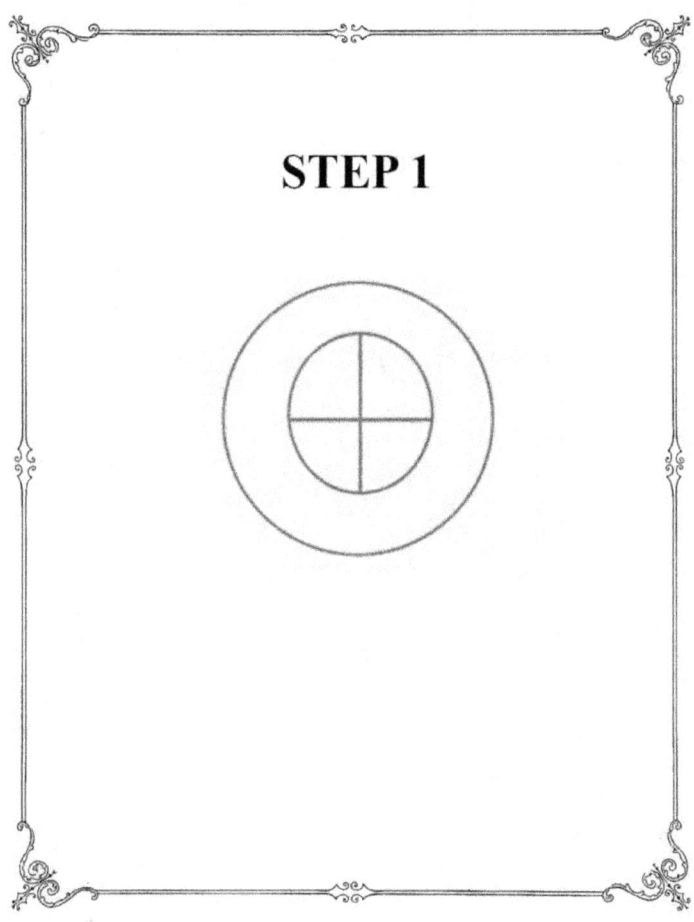

STEP 2

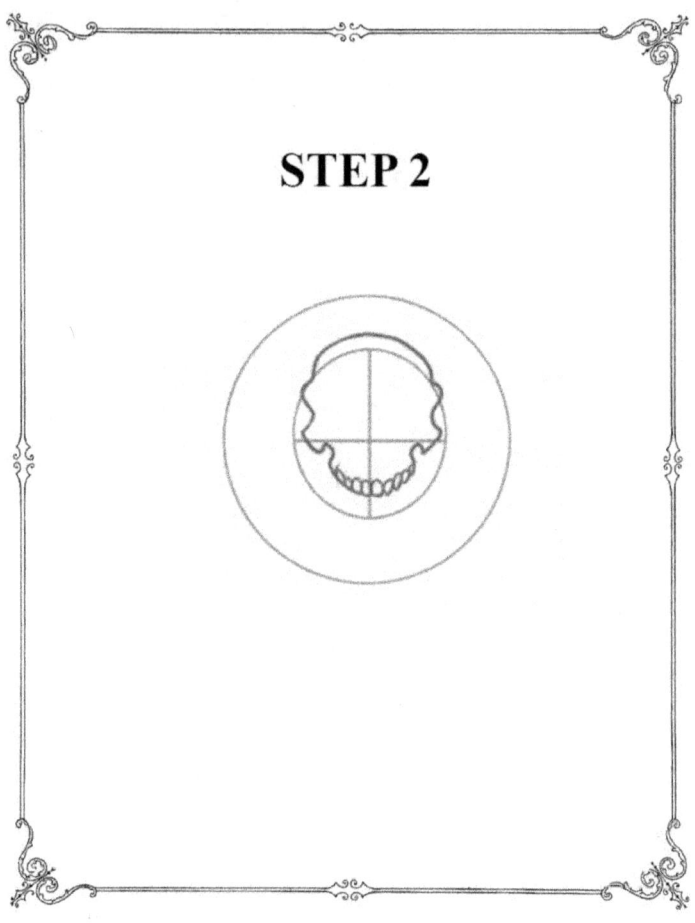

STEP 3

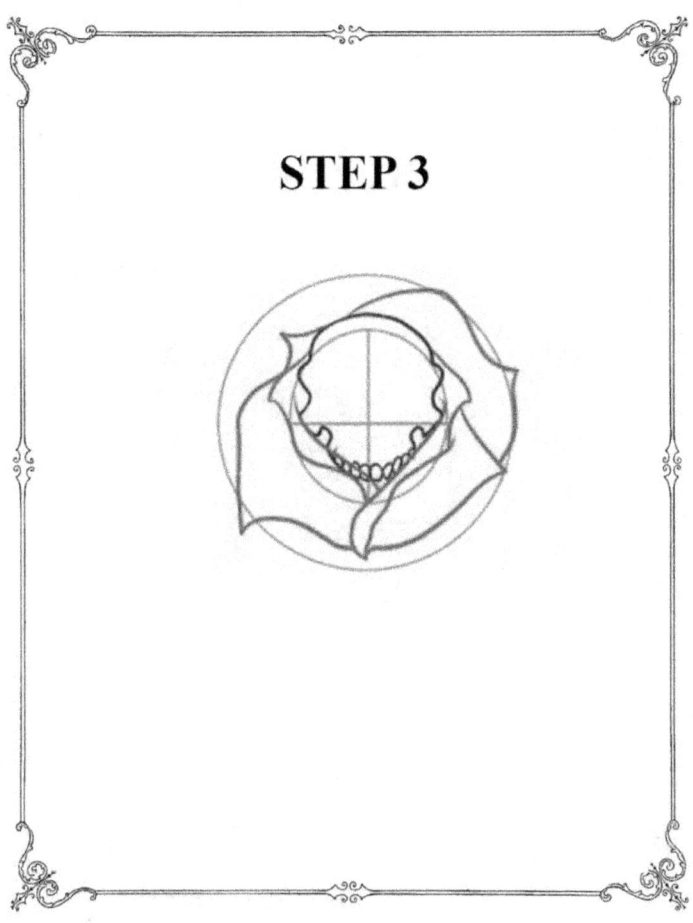

STEP 4

STEP 5

STEP 6

WAR SKULL

STEP 1

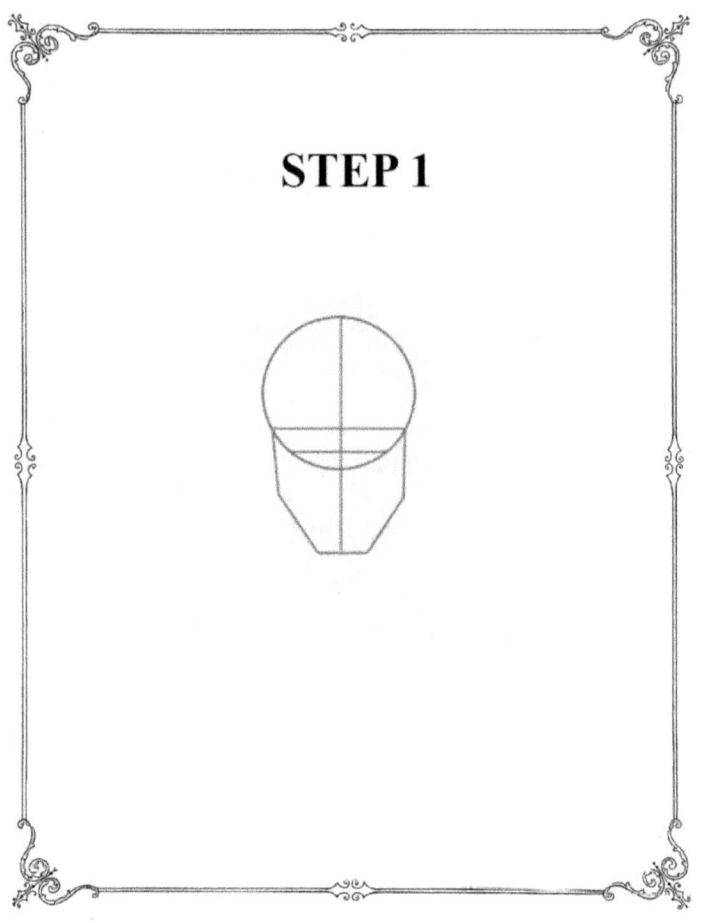

STEP 2

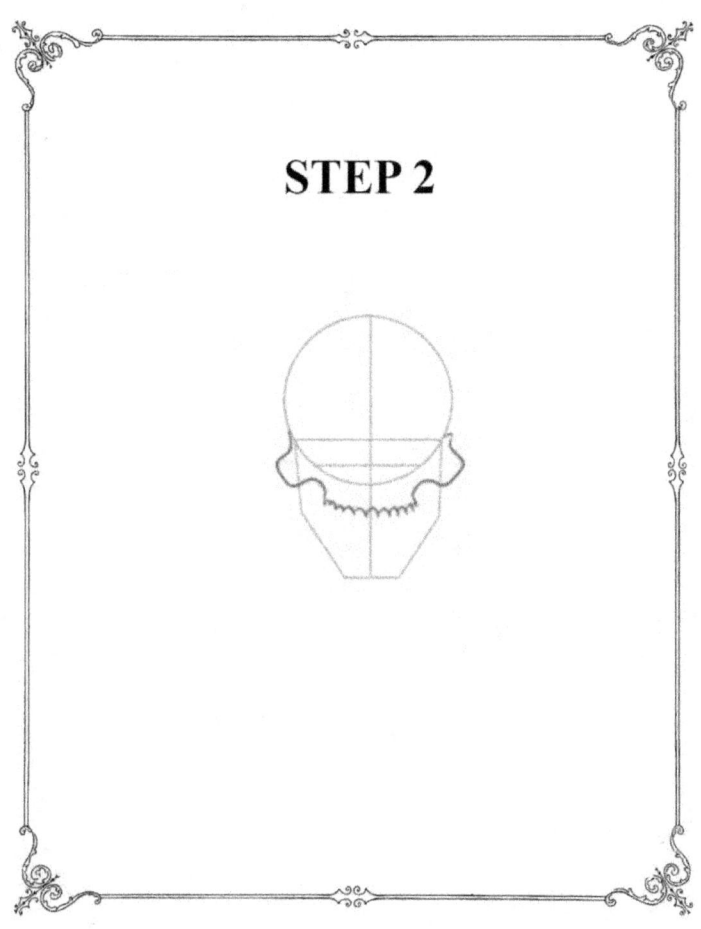

STEP 3

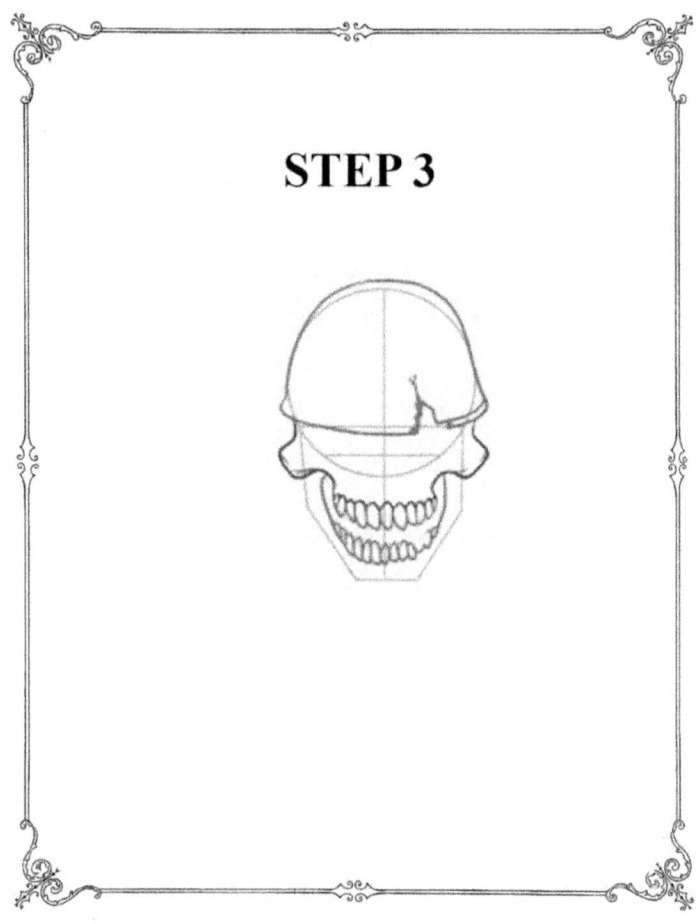

STEP 4

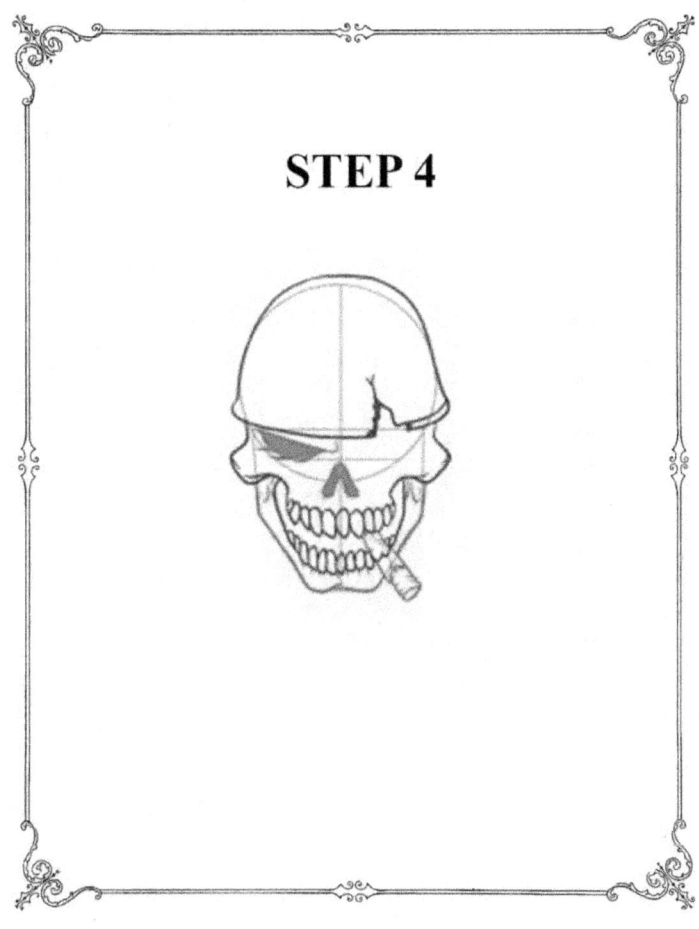

STEP 5

STEP 6

STEP 7

ZOMBIE SKULL

STEP 1

STEP 2

STEP 3

STEP 4

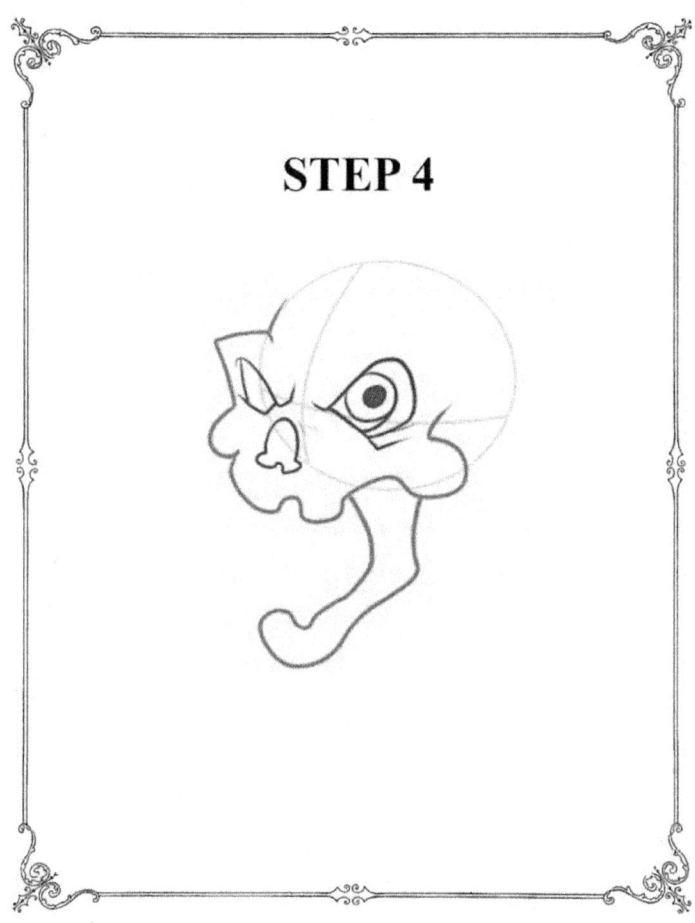

STEP 5

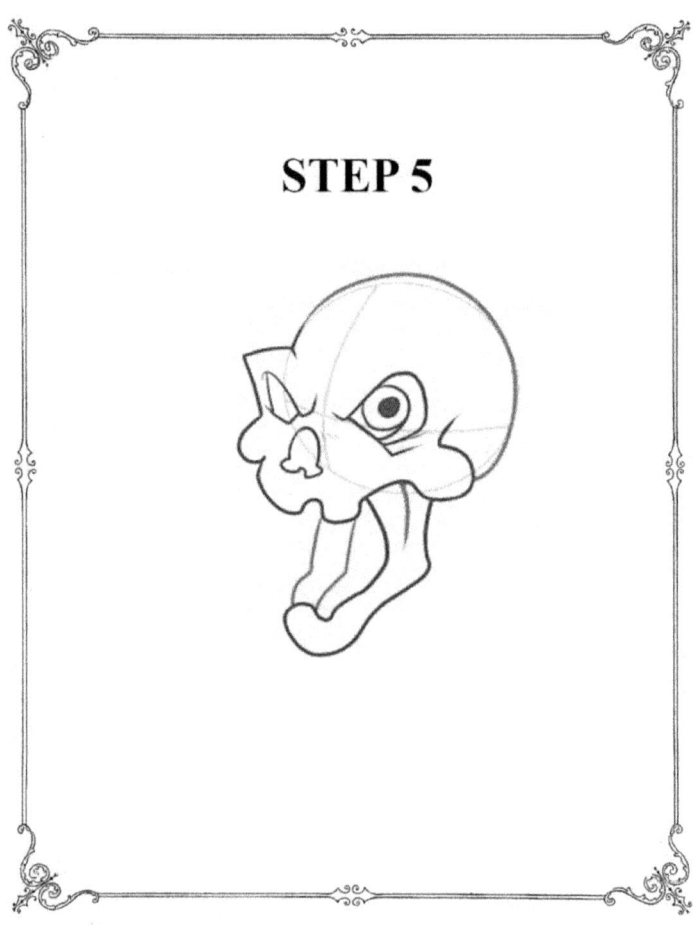

STEP 6

STEP 7